Glasgow Illustrated

George Fairfull Smith

Acknowledgements

The author is indebted to Glasgow City Council's Arts Development Fund for a research grant for the *Glasgow Illustrated* book and exhibition. Special thanks are also due to my family, colleagues and current and former members of Mitchell Library staff in the Glasgow Room, the Graphics, Photographic and Conservation departments, City Archives and the Typing Pool for all their help and advice. I am particularly grateful to Louise Boyle, Elizabeth Carmichael, Anne Escott, E.D.G.D. Fairfull-Smith, William J. Fairfull-Smith, Archie Fisher, David Freckleton, Ian Gordon, Cooper Hay, Andrew Jackson, Doreen Kean, Fionna MacPherson, Robert Miller, Cordelia Oliver, Enda Ryan, Hugh Stevenson, Katrina Thomson, Margaret Thomson, Moira Thorburn and Hamish Whyte.

George Fairfull Smith

Cover detail from *Glasgow*, drawn and lithographed by C. Stumpf and published by Schenck and Macfarlane of Edinburgh.

Published by Glasgow City Council Cultural and Leisure Services
1999

Printed by Cordfall Ltd. Glasgow

The Mitchell Library opened in 1877 and has grown to become one of Europe's largest public reference libraries. Its collection of material relating to Glasgow and its history is immense and ranges from the city's archives, maps, guidebooks, published histories and magazines, to ephemera, postcards, original works of art and newspapers. There are tens of thousands of topographical illustrations and portraits.

In addition to purchases the library has benefited from many gifts and bequests which have ensured that vital records of Glasgow's social, commercial and industrial history are preserved and made accessible to the widest public. These include the William Graham Collection of glass plate negatives, the Graham E. Langmuir Collection, which consists mainly of shipping material, the North British Locomotive Collection, William Young Scrap-books, the Wotherspoon Collection which records the rise and progress of shipbuilding on the Clyde, and the David Hamilton Collection, a pictorial survey of the work of one of the country's most influential architects.

There is a vast collection of views of Glasgow and its buildings which spans four centuries. The range of contemporary maps makes it possible to follow its development from a small community, built around the Molendinar Burn and Cathedral, to the great industrial and commercial centre of the nineteenth and early twentieth centuries. There is also a wide range of images of many of the small villages and towns which once were independent of Glasgow but were absorbed or obliterated by its expansion.

Many of these views were created by some of the city's most distinguished artists, engravers, photographers and publishers including William 'Crimean' Simpson, the first war artist, Joseph Swan, Thomas Fairbairn, Thomas Annan, Sir Muirhead Bone and Sir D.Y. Cameron.

In 1999 the library mounted *Glasgow Illustrated*, its first major exhibition reflecting the development of the city through four centuries. A selection of over three hundred and fifty images including prints, drawings, watercolours, postcards and photographs of cityscape, people, industry, rivers, transport and leisure activities, was chosen to reflect aspects of Glasgow's history and display the wealth and diversity of the Mitchell's collections.

Perhaps the least-known of all the material are the topographical views which are the subject of this publication.

Glasgow Illustrated from the Seventeenth to Twentieth Centuries

In the seventeenth century many visitors to Glasgow were impressed by its appearance. Thomas Morer wrote that it had 'the reputation of the finest town in Scotland, not excepting Edinburgh, tho' the royal city'. The two main streets were well-paved and surrounded by many new buildings with piazzas below them. Some of the earliest views date from this time and were made by John Slezer, a German artist, for *Theatrum Scotiae*, 1693. Slezer drew three scenes: *The Prospect of ye Town of Glasgow from ye South*, *The Colledge of Glasgow* and *The Prospect of ye Town of Glasgow from ye North East* (Fig. 1).

Daniel Defoe visited Glasgow early in the eighteenth century and wrote in his *Tour through the Whole Island of Great Britain*, 1724, 'in a word, 'tis the cleanest and beautifullest, and best built city in Britain'. In 1753 the Academy of the Fine Arts was established at the College, as the University was known, on the High Street. Its founders were Robert and Andrew Foulis, the renowned printers, who aimed to train artists and craftsmen and improve taste among the citizens of Glasgow. The library has an engraving of David Allan's view of the exhibition of Old Master paintings from the Academy's collection (Fig.2). It was held in the open air in the College's inner court. Some of the paintings, prints and drawings produced by the pupils were advertised for sale. There were several by Robert Paul including *Glasgow from the south*, *St. Andrew's Church* and the *Middle Walk in the College Garden* (Fig.3). His most famous work, *The Trongate* (Fig.4), was completed after his death by William Buchanan, a fellow pupil. It shows the elegant buildings and piazzas which impressed so many visitors. The original prints created at the Foulis Academy are extremely rare and facsimile sets were published by William Gemmell in *Early Views of Glasgow*, 1913.

Glasgow's reputation was further enhanced by the numerous artists who drew, etched and engraved the town and its major buildings to illustrate a range of publications. Many followed Slezer and Paul by choosing to replicate the view from the south bank of the River Clyde. John Clerk of Eldin's *View of Glasgow from Windmill Croft*, 1773, from *Etchings chiefly of views in Scotland*, 1825, spans from the Windmill, south-west of the town, to the Glasgow Bridge, spires of the old Hutchesons' Hospital and Merchants' House on the north bank, and includes the sailing vessels on the river.

Buildings and other structures in and around Glasgow provided ideal subject matter. The Cathedral was an obvious choice for artists including Paul Sandby in *A Collection of one hundred and fifty select views in England, Wales, Scotland and Ireland, 1782–3* (Fig.5). The *Kelvin Aqueduct Bridge*, carrying the Forth and Clyde Canal, was drawn by John Claude

Nattes and engraved by Merigot to illustrate John Stoddart's *Remarks on local scenery and manners in Scotland during the years 1799 and 1800*, 1801; Adam de Cardonnel etched the castles of *Cruixton* (Crookston) (Fig.6) and *Cathcart* for *Picturesque Antiquities of Scotland*, 1788.

These views of Glasgow and its buildings, in conjunction with contemporary maps, provide valuable information. The earliest map, albeit small-scale, appears in Blaeu's *Atlas*, 1694. Later plans such as John McArthur's *Plan of the City of Glasgow, Gorbells, and Calton*, 1778, detail most of the important streets and buildings. They help to trace Glasgow's growth from its medieval precincts around the Molendinar and Cathedral, southward down the High Street to the Trongate and Glasgow Cross. Many show the outlying villages and communities such as Gorbals and Little Govan on the south side of the River Clyde.

In addition to maps and plans, published histories help to recreate how Glasgow looked at the end of the eighteenth century. Four had been published by this time including John McUre's *The city of Glasgow; or, an account of its origin, rise and progress, with a more particular description thereof than has hitherto been known*, 1736, John Gibson's *History of Glasgow from the earliest accounts to the present time*, 1777, and Andrew Brown's two-volume *History of Glasgow, Paisley, Greenock and Port Glasgow*, 1795–7.

The most important was James Denholm's *An historical account and topographical description of the city of Glasgow and suburbs*, 1797. It featured a plan and eleven illustrations drawn by Denholm and engraved by Robert Scott of Edinburgh.

The closing decades of the century saw the construction of several important public buildings by Robert and James Adam: the Infirmary next to the Cathedral, Assembly Rooms on Ingram Street and Trades' Hall on Glassford Street. Denholm discussed and illustrated them along with *St. Enoch's Square with the church and Surgeons' Hall* (Fig.7), and the *Army Barracks on the north side of the Gallowgate*. His view of the square shows the eighteenth-century St. Enoch's Church which was demolished and replaced by another building. The later church is the subject of a print made by Marjorie Bates in the early twentieth century (Fig.8).

Two further editions of Denholm's work were published in 1798 and 1804 with additional illustrations including a *View of Glasgow from the South* (Fig.9) and the new *Theatre Royal* on Queen Street (Fig.10) which was designed by David Hamilton and opened to the public in 1805. Other early views owned by the library include two drawings by unknown artists: the *Broomielaw of Glasgow*, 1807 (Fig.11), and the *Molendinar and Cathedral* (Fig.12).

Denholm's publisher was Robert Chapman who also produced *The Picture of Glasgow; or, stranger's guide* which went through several editions from 1806 to 1822. The first one had no illustrations but did have a fold-out plan. Subsequent editions included a view of *Carlton Place* (Fig.13), the fashionable terrace on the south bank of the River Clyde. Another popular guidebook was *Glasgow Delineated*, published in four editions from 1821 to 1836. The engravings included the *Glasgow Horse Bazaar* on Union Street and the *Canal Office, Port Dundas*, both engraved by Robert Scott.

The 1820s also saw the publication of two very important works in Glasgow. In 1825 *The Glasgow Looking Glass*, a four-page satirical magazine later called the *Northern Looking Glass*, was printed lithographically. It was lavishly illustrated by William Heath and encompassed a wide range of subjects reflecting life in early nineteenth-century Glasgow. These included fashions, a promenade in the Royal Botanical Garden in Sandyford, north of Sauchiehall Street, classes at Anderson's and the Mechanics' Institutions and the Glasgow Fair, perhaps the most famous image from this short-lived publication.

In 1826 Joseph Swan, an engraver in the city, published the first in his series of *Select Views of Glasgow and its Environs*. John M. Leighton wrote the historical and descriptive text and the engravings were made from drawings by John Fleming, John Knox and Swan himself. The entire work was completed by 1828. The views include *George Square* (Fig.14), *Port Dundas from Garnet Hill* (Fig.15), *Glasgow from Little Govan* and *Buchanan Street*. Following its success Swan commenced the publication of *Select Views on the River Clyde*. Leighton provided the text and the series was critically acclaimed. One of the finest illustrations is Andrew Donaldson's *Clyde at Govan from the east* (Fig.16) which shows the steeple of Govan Church. Leighton noted that visitors from the south had compared the town to Stratford-upon-Avon.

Swan's publications were very successful but some believed their price placed them outwith the reach of many people. In 1834 the first issue of *Glasgow Illustrated in a Series of Picturesque Views* was praised for its lower cost which made it more accessible. The text was by John Gullan, who taught English and geography in the city. Glasgow's John Scott drew and engraved the illustrations. They included a view of the city from the Merchants' Park (now the Necropolis), the *Assembly Rooms* (Fig.17) and the *Cathedral from the Washing Green* which was criticised for its inappropriate viewpoint.

The following year Allan and Ferguson, soon to become one of the city's most important businesses, published *Views in Glasgow and Neighbourhood*. Leighton supplied the text and the drawings, which were almost all by James Anderson, were lithographed by David Allan, one of the firm's partners. This volume highlights some of the surrounding towns and countryside such as *Govan*, the *Clyde, below Govan* and *Partick* (Figs.18–20).

Although James Anderson is not credited for the artwork, some years later William Simpson, one of his contemporaries at Allan and Ferguson, revealed him to be the artist in his own memoirs. While with the firm Simpson produced most of the drawings which were lithographed and published in *Views and Notices of Glasgow in Former Times*, 1848. The accompanying text was written by Robert Stuart. The book contains views by other artists including Weir's *Part of the Archbishop's Palace and St. Nicholas' Chapel* (Fig.21) and John Hart's fascinating late eighteenth-century drawings of *Argyle Street* and *Grahamston* (Fig.22), the village that was destroyed for the construction of Central Station. Allan and Fergsuon also published a wide range of prints of Glasgow views including James Anderson's *Glasgow Bridge* (Fig.23), and a series of vignettes which subsequently were included in James Pagan's *Sketch of the History of Glasgow*, 1847.

The 1840s were a particularly busy time for artists and publishers. In addition to his work in *Views and Notices…*, William Simpson made a series of drawings in and around the city. He worked them up to finished watercolours which were acquired by Glasgow Art Gallery and Museum and published in 1899 in *Glasgow in the "Forties"*. They were restored and redisplayed in the People's Palace in 1998.

The Mitchell has three albums containing many of Simpson's sketches for *Glasgow in the "Forties"* and other works. These include a group of very important early views of Glasgow's industry and shipbuilding such as *Port Dundas near the Timber Basin, New Quay on the south side, Napier's building yard, Kelvinhaugh slip-dock,* and *Dixon's Iron Works* (Figs. 24–28). He also recorded many famous landmarks such as *Garscadden Gates, James Watt's House, Delftfield* and the *Old House opposite the Barony* (Figs.29–31), better known as the Provand's Lordship. James Thomson's print (Fig.32) provides an atmospheric view of the same building. The albums also have work by some of Simpson's contemporaries including *Rocks at the Pear Tree Well* (Fig.33), a particularly fine watercolour by Robert Carrick, and John Hart's drawings of Argyle Street. Other watercolours by Simpson in the library's collection include *Glasgow Cross* and *Gorbals Steeple* (Figs.34 & 35).

Thomas Fairbairn was another watercolour artist whose work was reproduced in major publications. James Bogle, Lord Dean of Guild, commissioned him to paint twenty-one watercolour drawings of old Glasgow which were lithographed and published by Miller and

Buchanan in *Relics of Ancient Architecture and other Picturesque Scenes in Glasgow*, 1849. They include the *Old Stockwell Bridge* (Fig.36), *Avenue in the Green* (Fig.37), *Ladywell Street and the Cathedral* and the *Old Baronial Hall, Gorbals*. The original works are also in the People's Palace and in 1885 a new edition of *Relics of Ancient Architecture and other Picturesque Scenes in Glasgow* was published with these and additional drawings by Fairbairn.

The artists and publishers illustrated historic and contemporary events as well as views of the town and riverscapes. In December 1846 the Glasgow Philosophical Society opened a large exhibition of arts and manufactures in the City Hall (Fig.38). It attracted almost 100,000 visitors over fifteen days. Twenty years later the Industrial Exhibition was equally popular (Fig.39). A view of the *Defence of the Cathedral by the Trades' House in 1579 during the Reformation* (Fig.40) by David Roberts, the renowned Scottish artist, was published in *Scotland Delineated,* 1847–54. Queen Victoria visited the city in 1849 and several artists and publishers recorded the historic day. Maclure and Macdonald, lithographers to the Queen, whose business was equal to that of Allan and Ferguson, published a series of views including *The Landing, The Triumphal Arch* and *The Trongate* (Fig.41). The accompanying text was by James Hedderwick.

In addition to the three albums of drawings by William Simpson and his contemporaries the library owns other topographical views by Glasgow artists. A small group has been attributed to Robert Carrick and includes *Kelvinbridge looking towards Great Western Road, Clyde Street from the east* (Figs.42 & 43), *St. Vincent Crescent* and *Cathedral Square*. Alexander Duff Robertson, an influential art teacher in Glasgow, is represented by *Three Tree Well* and *Cottage, Kelvingrove* (Figs.44 & 45). There are pencil drawings by William Young, one of his pupils, such as the *View of the Kelvin Flint Mills* and *Old Houses in Byres Road* (Fig.46). Work by Alexander Shanks includes *The Trongate* (Fig.47), painted *c.*1850.

The advent of photography in the mid-nineteenth century provided new opportunities and the work of several pioneers can be found in the collections. John Urie was one of Glasgow's leading commercial photographers and the library owns his portraits of Madeleine Smith and Pierre L'Angelier, her ill-fated lover. An advert for his business in Buchanan Street is preserved in the William Young Scrapbooks.

Thomas Annan is the best-known of all the city's nineteenth-century photographers. He trained with Joseph Swan as an engraver but realised photography's potential and set up in business in the 1850s. His work encompassed a wide range of subjects including portraits, landscape, ships on the Clyde, Glasgow's townscape and major events such as the construction and completion of the Loch Katrine Waterworks. In the 1860s he produced a series of views for *Photographs of Glasgow* which has text by the Rev. A.G. Forbes. Two copies of this publication reveal that Annan updated his work. In one the view of the Cathedral includes the row of houses on Castle Street beyond the old Infirmary. The later photograph shows John Honeyman's Barony Free Church which replaced them.

Annan's most famous work commenced in 1868 when he was commissioned by the City Improvement Trust to photograph the slums of Glasgow's old town which were due for demolition. The dark and narrow closes off the High Street and Saltmarket could be difficult to photograph but he overcame the problems and produced an important and sensitive account of the terrible living conditions. The work was published in *Old Closes and Streets of Glasgow*.

Several of Annan's stark photographs can be directly compared and contrasted with watercolour views of the same locations by contemporary artists such as William Simpson's earlier *Old Houses on the High Street* (Figs.48 & 49), Patrick Downie's *Laigh Kirk Close* (Figs.50 & 51), and David Small's *28 Saltmarket* (Figs.52 & 53). Small's *Old Houses, Main Street, Gorbals* (Fig.54) makes an interesting comparison with Annan's *Main Street Gorbals, Looking South* (Fig.55). William Simpson's earlier sketch of the *Interior of the old Baronial Hall* in the Gorbals is a valuable record of a famous landmark (Fig.56).

Among other works by Patrick Downie are *Union Court, off Rottenrow* (Fig.57), *Old Close in the Bridgegate* and *Calton*. There are over twenty watercolours by Small which range from the *Corner of North Street and Main Street, Anderston* and the *Corner of Taylor Street and Rottenrow* (Figs.58 & 59) to *Lord Darnley's Cottage, Broomielaw,* and *Old Houses, Kelvinside*. Some of the pictures in the collection relate to his drawings which were reproduced in *Sketches of Quaint Bits in Glasgow still standing in the year 1885*, 1887 and *By-gone Glasgow..*, 1896.

Another Glasgow photographer whose work overlaps the nineteenth and twentieth centuries is William Graham. His range of interests is reflected in the diversity of subject matter from people to Glasgow's historic sites and relics including the old Ship Bank building on the Bridgegate, Tolbooth Bell and Gorbals Foundry. His collection consists of over three thousand images.

The firm established by Thomas Annan continued under the name of T. and R. Annan & Sons and survives to the present day. A view of *Glasgow Harbour from the south*, 1892 (Fig.60), shows many notable landmarks including Jamaica Bridge which Harold Storey painted just over twenty years later (Fig.61). Robert Eadie's *Glasgow Quay* (Fig.62) is another valuable record of the riverside.

Although photography replaced the work of many artists and illustrators in publications, printmaking techniques continued to be used by leading artists in Glasgow. D.Y. Cameron produced an evocative series of etchings which were published in *The Regality Club*, 1893–1912. They include *Old Houses, Rottenrow, Old Houses, Byres Road, Elphinstone Tower and Chapel* (Figs.63–65) and *David Dale's House, Charlotte Street*. Muirhead Bone also created some of the most atmospheric views of the city's streets, buildings and industries. In 1911 subjects such as *Queen's Dock, Glasgow University from Cessnock Dock* (Figs.66 & 67), *Kelvinhaugh Ferry*, and *Saturday Barrow Market* were published in *Glasgow: Fifty Drawings*. Forty-six of the illustrations were engraved in photogravure by the city's T. and R. Annan and Sons.

The collection of twentieth-century photographs has been enhanced by the work of John Logan, Michael Smith, George Oliver and other practitioners. Logan's *Cross Keys Inn, Rottenrow* (Fig.68) records a well-known landmark, now demolished. It is part of a valuable resource which provides information on areas of the city which were devastated by redevelopment in the 1960s. Photographs of districts such as Pollokshaws on the south side are complemented by artists' prints including A.P. Thomson's *Pollokshaws Town House* (Fig.69).

The Mitchell Library's collections continue to grow and reflect many aspects of the city. Their accessibility enriches anyone with an interest in the history of Glasgow.

Fig. 1   John Slezer, *The Prospect of ye Town of Glasgow from ye North East*, from *Theatrum Scotiae*, 1693.

Fig.2   David Allan, *Foulis Academy Exhibition, Inner Court of the Old College*, 1761, print.

Fig. 3   Robert Paul, *View of the Middle Walk in the College Garden*, 1756, print.

Fig. 4   Robert Paul and William Buchanan, *The Trongate*, 1770, print.

Fig. 5   Paul Sandby, *Cathedral from the south-west*, 1780, from *A Collection of one hundred and fifty select views in England, Wales, Scotland and Ireland*, 1782–3.

Fig. 6   Adam de Cardonnel, *Cruixton Castle*, from *Picturesque Antiquities of Scotland*, 1788.

Fig. 7   James Denholm and Robert Scott, *St. Enoch's Square with the church and Surgeons' Hall*, from *An historical account and topographical description of the city of Glasgow and suburbs*, 1797.

Fig. 8   Marjorie Bates, *St. Enoch's Church*, print.

Fig. 9   James Denholm and Robert Scott, *View of Glasgow from the South*, from
          The History of the City of Glasgow and Suburbs, 1804.

Fig. 10   James Denholm and Robert Scott, *Theatre Royal*, from *The History of the City of Glasgow and Suburbs*, 1804.

Fig. 11   Artist unknown, *Broomielaw of Glasgow*, 1807, drawing.

Fig. 12   Artist unknown, *Molendinar and Cathedral*, watercolour.

Fig. 13   W. Reid and Robert Scott, *Carlton Place*, from *The Picture of Glasgow; or, stranger's guide*, 1812.

Fig. 14 John Fleming and Joseph Swan, *George Square*, from *Select Views of Glasgow and its Environs*, 1828.

Fig. 15   Joseph Swan, *Port Dundas from Garnet Hill*, from *Select Views of Glasgow and its Environs*, 1828.

Fig. 16   Andrew Donaldson and Joseph Swan, *Clyde at Govan from the east,* from *Select Views on the River Clyde,* 1830.

Fig. 17   John Scott, *Assembly Rooms*, from *Glasgow Illustrated in a Series of Picturesque Views,* 1834.

Fig. 18   James Anderson and David Allan, *Govan*, from *Views in Glasgow and Neighbourhood*, 1835.

Fig. 19   James Anderson and David Allan, *Clyde, below Govan*, from *Views in Glasgow and Neighbourhood*, 1835.

Fig. 20   James Anderson and David Allan, *Partick*, from *Views in Glasgow and Neighbourhood*, 1835.

Fig. 21   Weir, *Part of the Archbishop's Palace and St. Nicholas' Chapel*, from *Views and Notices of Glasgow in Former Times*, 1848.

Fig. 22   John Hart, *Argyle Street* (top) and *Grahamston* (bottom), from *Views and Notices of Glasgow in Former Times*, 1848.

Fig. 23   James Anderson, *Glasgow Bridge*, print.

Fig. 24   William Simpson, *Port Dundas near the Timber Basin*, *c.*1850, watercolour.

Within the image (handwritten):

10 June 1848

New Quay on South Side opposite Napiers Wet Docks, with Remains of Tod & McGregors building Yards 10th July 18--

Wm Simpson

Fig. 25   William Simpson, *New Quay on the south side of the River Clyde*, 1848, watercolour.

Fig. 26   William Simpson, *Govan, with Napier's building yard*, 1845, watercolour.

Kelvinhaugh Slip-dock on North Side of Clyde.
East End of Govan. date about 1845. Wm Simpson. 29. April.

Fig. 27 William Simpson, *Kelvinhaugh slip-dock from the east end of Govan*, 1845, watercolour.

Fig. 28   William Simpson, *Sketch near Dixon's Iron Works, c.*1850,watercolour.

Fig. 29   William Simpson, *Garscadden Gates near Maryhill*, *c.*1844, watercolour.

Drawn by Wm Simpson   Sketched about 1847. or 1848.

Fig. 30   William Simpson, *James Watt's House, Delftfield Lane* (now James Watt Street), *c.*1847–48, watercolour.

Fig. 31   William Simpson, *Old House opposite the Barony*, 1843, watercolour.

Fig. 32   James Thomson, *Provand's Lordship*, print.

Fig. 33   Robert Carrick, *Rocks at the Pear Tree Well*, 1840, watercolour.

Fig. 34   William Simpson, *Glasgow Cross*, 1850, watercolour.

Fig. 35   William Simpson, *Gorbals Steeple from the Old Brig*, 1845, watercolour.

Fig. 36   Thomas Fairbairn, *Old Stockwell Bridge*, from *Relics of Ancient Architecture
and other Picturesque Scenes in Glasgow*, 1849.

Fig. 37   Thomas Fairbairn, *Avenue in the Green*, from *Relics of Ancient Architecture and other Picturesque Scenes in Glasgow*, 1849.

Fig. 38   View of the interior of the City Hall during the Glasgow Philosophical Society's Exhibition, 1846–7, print.

Fig. 39   View of the Industrial Exhibition, Glasgow, from the *Illustrated London News*, January 1866.

Fig. 40   David Roberts and J.D. Harding, *Defence of the Cathedral by the Trades' House in 1579 during the Reformation*, from *Scotland Delineated*, 1847–54.

Fig. 41   Maclure and Macdonald, *The Trongate*, from *Queen Victoria at Glasgow*, 1849.

Fig. 42   Attributed to Robert Carrick, *Kelvinbridge looking towards Great Western Road*, *c.*1852, drawing.

Fig. 43   Attributed to Robert Carrick, *Clyde Street from the east*, *c*.1850, drawing.

Fig. 44   Alexander Duff Robertson, *Three Tree Well, Kelvingrove*, 1853, watercolour.

Fig. 45   Alexander Duff Robertson, *Cottage, Kelvingrove*, 1841, drawing.

Fig. 46   William Young, *View of the Kelvin Flint Mills and North Woodside House*, 1868 (top), and *Old Houses in Byres Road, Partick*, 1868 (bottom), drawings.

Fig. 47   Alexander Shanks, *The Trongate*, *c.*1850, watercolour.

Fig. 48 Thomas Annan, *Old Buildings, High Street*, 1868, from *Old Closes and Streets of Glasgow*.

Fig. 49   William Simpson, *Old Houses on the High Street*, from *Views and Notices of Glasgow in Former Times*, 1848.

Fig. 50   Thomas Annan, Laigh
Kirk Close, 1868, from
*Old Closes and Streets
of Glasgow*.

Fig. 51   Patrick Downie, *Laigh Kirk Close*,
           1890, watercolour.

Fig. 52 Thomas Annan, *28 Saltmarket*, 1868, from *Old Closes and Streets of Glasgow*.

Fig. 53   David Small, *28 Saltmarket*, 1864, watercolour.

Fig. 54   David Small, *Old Houses, Main Street, Gorbals*, 1875, watercolour.

Fig. 55   Thomas Annan, *Main Street Gorbals Looking South*, 1868, from *Old Closes and Streets of Glasgow*.

Fig. 56 William Simpson, *Baronial Hall, Gorbals: interior of drinking-room*, 1858, watercolour.

Fig. 57   Patrick Downie, *Union Court, off Rottenrow*, 1891, watercolour.

Fig. 58   David Small, *Corner of North Street and Main Street, Anderston*, 1882, watercolour.

Fig. 59   David Small, *Corner of Taylor Street and Rottenrow*, 1864, watercolour.

Fig. 60   T. & R. Annan & Sons, *Glasgow Harbour from the south*, 1892.

Fig. 61   Harold Storey, *Jamaica Bridge*, 1913, watercolour.

Fig. 62 Robert Eadie, *Glasgow Quay from the south side of Stockwell Bridge*, watercolour.

Fig. 63   D.Y. Cameron, *Old Houses, Rottenrow*, from *The Regality Club*, 1899.

Fig. 64   D.Y. Cameron, *Old Houses, Byres Road*, 1894, from *The Regality Club*, 1899.

Fig. 65   D.Y. Cameron, *Elphinstone Tower and Chapel*, from *The Regality Club*, 1912.

Fig. 66   Muirhead Bone, *Queen's Dock*, from *Glasgow: Fifty Drawings*, 1911.

Fig. 67 Muirhead Bone, *Glasgow University from Cessnock Dock*, from *Glasgow: Fifty Drawings*, 1911.

Fig. 68   John Logan, *Cross Keys Inn, Rottenrow*.

Fig. 69 A.P. Thomson, *Pollokshaws Town House*, print.

Glasgow Illustrators

Glasgow Illustrated features the work of a wide range of artists, engravers, publishers and photographers many of whom were born in the city or lived there.

Some of the earliest views were produced by Robert Paul (1739–70) and David Allan (1744–96). Both were pupils at Glasgow's Foulis Academy which predated the Royal Academy in London. James Denholm (1772–1818) wrote *An historical account and topographical description of the city of Glasgow and suburbs,* 1797, the first illustrated guide to Glasgow. His drawings were engraved by Lanark-born Robert Scott (1777–1841) from Edinburgh.

Select Views of Glasgow and its Environs, 1828, was published and engraved by Joseph Swan (1796–1872) with illustrations by Glasgow's John Knox (1778–1845), Greenock-based John Fleming (1792–1845) and Swan himself. John Gullan's *Glasgow Illustrated in a Series of Picturesque Views,* 1834, features the work of John Scott (*fl.*1820s–30s). The illustrations in *Views in Glasgow and Neighbourhood,* 1835, were drawn by James Anderson (*fl.*1830s) and lithographed by David Allan (1809–75) of Allan and Ferguson.

Robert Stuart's *Views and Notices of Glasgow in Former Times,* 1848, was illustrated by Glasgow-born William Simpson (1823–99) and the three albums of Simpson's drawings in the library also contain work by James Anderson and Robert Carrick (1820–1905) who worked with Simpson at Allan and Ferguson.

Alexander Duff Robertson (1807–86) was a notable watercolourist who taught at the Mechanics' Institution and the Glasgow Government School of Design, precursor of Glasgow School of Art. William Young (1845–1916) was one of his pupils and a co-founder of the Glasgow Art Club. Young's Scrapbooks in the library's Glasgow Collection are an invaluable source for local historians.

Sir David Young Cameron (1865–1945) was born in Glasgow and became a renowned painter, watercolourist and etcher. Sir Muirhead Bone (1876–1953) was born in Partick and studied at Glasgow School of Art. Greenock-born Patrick Downie (1854–1945) lived in Glasgow and painted watercolours of the old streets and closes around the High Street. David Small (1846–1927) was chief artist for the *Dundee Advertiser* and painted views of buildings and streetscapes across Scotland.

Glasgow's famous and influential photographers include Thomas Annan (1829–87) who recorded the old streets and closes around the High Street, and William Graham (1845–1914) whose photographs of Springburn are of particular interest.

The Mitchell Library's resources can provide further information on many of the individuals who illustrated Glasgow.